Finger Knitting Projects

Simple and Amazing Finger Knitting Patterns Everyone Can do

DEDICATION

Contents

Chunky Finger-Knit Pillow

Materials

2 skeins of different colored yarn (I used Lion Brand Wool-Ease Thick and Quick in Bold Pea Green and Natural Cream)

14" x 14" pillow form

1/2 yard of canvas/duck cloth

coordinating thread

long tapestry needle

sewing machine

Instructions

1. Finger knit two skeins of yarn in colors of your choosing. The finger knitting will finish as one long strand.

2. Lay out a piece of canvas/duck cloth that is 20" x 18", using the 20" side as your width. Pin the ends of the finger-knitting strands side by side at the top of the canvas.

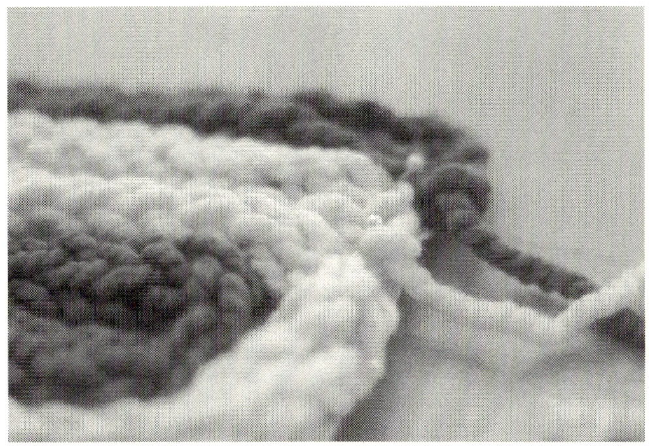

3. Keeping the strands side by side, bring the lengths of finger knitting across the width of the canvas, turn and bring them back again, pinning the lengths into place as you go. The colors will alternate as you turn the lengths at each side. The front side of the finger knitting has what looks like side-by-side chain stitches; keep these facing up. The back side looks more like a ladder. Keep this side of the finger knitting oriented down to the canvas, so that your strands of finger knitting look smooth, not twisted.

4. Your fully pinned finger knitting should look as follows. In my photo, the canvas extends beyond 20" horizontally, but 20" will be enough.

5. Now with a sewing machine, affix the lengths of finger knitting to the canvas by sewing vertically along the edge of the pillow, about 2 1/2 inches in from the side. (A 100 size needle or stronger is best; however, I used a size 90 needle just fine.) Use your fingers to press the finger knitting under the foot of the sewing machine as you go.

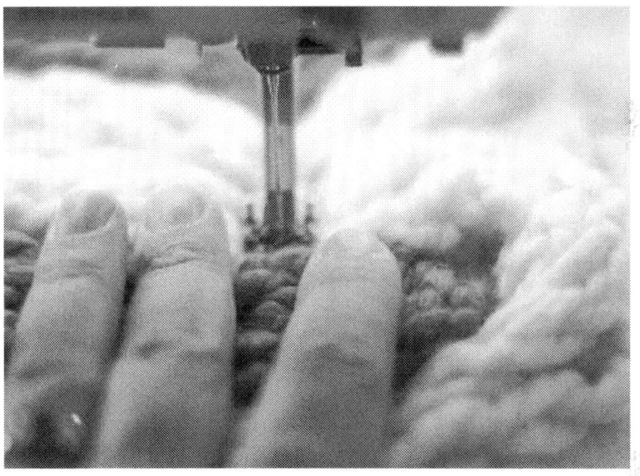

6. Your stitching on each side of the piece should be approximately 14.5" to 15" apart. Make sure to sew through the finger knitting before the coil starts to turn so that the strands are straight as they go into the pillow.

7. Take another piece of the canvas, at least 16" x 16", and draw a 14.5" x 14.5" square on it with a pencil or light marking pen (this will be on the inside of the pillow).

8. Place this piece of canvas face to face with the finger knitting, keeping the marked square facing up toward you.

9. Pin the canvas into place, making an effort to place the sewing line at the top and bottom of the pillow such that, a) the stripes come out even, and b) that when you sew along that line, you will be sewing directly through the middle of a strand of finger knitting.

10. Sew along the marked line, leaving a 6" length along the side of the pillow unstitched to make room to turn the pillow inside out and to get the pillow form inside.

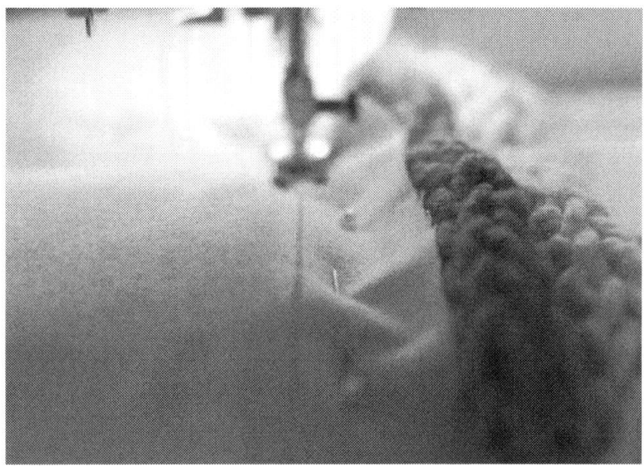

11. Turn the pillow right side out by reaching through the opening along the side and pulling the pillow through. Make sure the lengths of finger knitting and stripes are the way you want them. Now's the time to adjust stitching, if needed.

12. Turn the pillow back inside out and trim all the edges to approximately 5/8", clipping the corners of the pillow almost to the seam line.

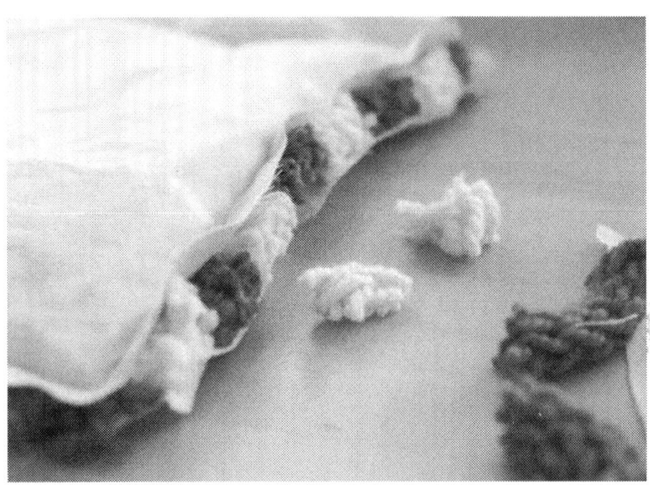

13. Turn the pillow inside out again, and stuff it with the pillow form through the unstitched opening.

14. After the pillow form is in, hand-sew the opening closed using the ladder stitch. Start the needle and thread by securing it in the opening as close to the machine stitching as possible. Make a small stitch by bringing the needle through the fold of the fabric (as below). Then bring the needle to the other side, directly across from where your needle came out and make a small stitch through the fold on the finger-knitting side. Repeat this stitch over and over until you sew the entire opening closed. Finish off the thread.

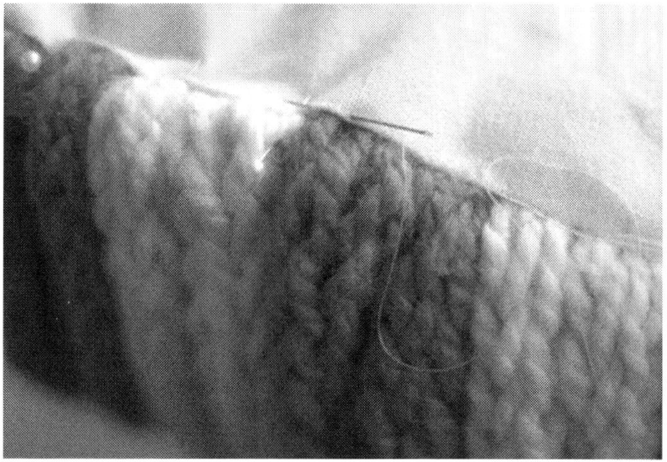

15. Now orient your strands of finger knitting on the pillow and tack them down in place using a long tapestry needle. I took long running stitches through the pillow and short stitches in the top so they wouldn't be seen. Tacking down the strands will ensure the stripes are even and there is no gapping.

That's it, you're finished!

Finger Knit Pouf

Materials

Loopity Loops Yarn (2 1/2 skeins)

Darning needle

White or complimenting yarn

Fiberfill/pillow stuffing

Instructions

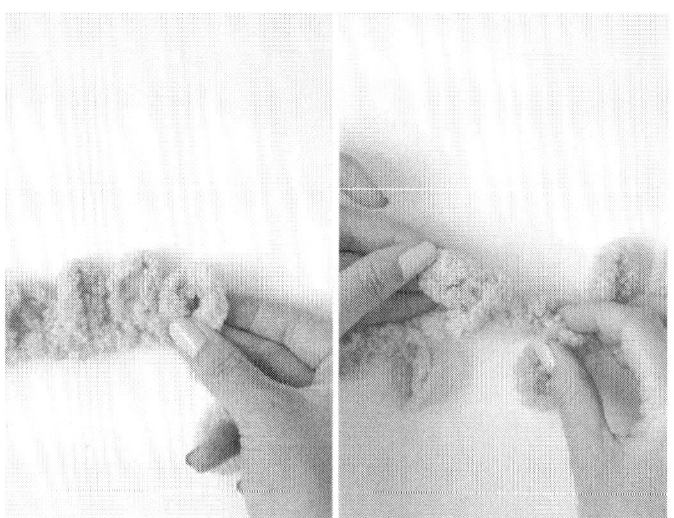

1. Step 1: Find the end and pull out a long section of yarn. With the loops facing up, count 30 across.
2. Step 2: Pull the 31st loop through the 30th one in order to create the second row. Continue across the 30 loops, then go back the other way, continuing to pull the working yarn loops up through the existing loops.

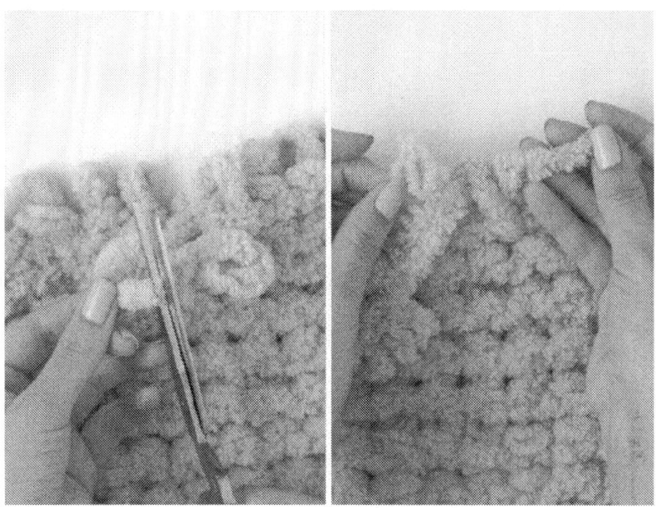

3. Step 3: When you eventually reach the end of one skein, cut one of the loops so that you have a small piece of straight yarn. Weave this through the loops. Then do the same with a new skein and continue the pattern where you left off (similar to crochet).

Note, it's easy to miss a loop here and there, so check your work after each row to make sure you've looped everything through. If you make a mistake, you can simply pull the loops free to fix it. It's a quick fix!

4. Step 4: When you've finished about 2 1/2 skeins of yarn, stop and DO NOT cut the yarn yet. The length of the piece will be the entire circumference of the pouf, so the longer it is, the wider around the pouf will be.

5. Step 5: Join the two ends of the piece. Note, one side of the piece will have a different look than the other (a front and a back). Whichever side you want facing OUT, put those two sides together.

6. Step 6: With one hand, group the open loop of one end with the already knitted loops of the opposite end. With the working yarn in the other hand, pull the next loop through both openings to bind the sides together. Repeat with the next loop and all the way across the piece.

7. Step 7: To finish the loops and prevent unraveling of your pouf, take the left loop and pull it through the right loop. Do this only once. Then take the new right loop and pull it through the left loop. Continue this pattern all the way across the final set of loops in order to bind them together in a chain-like stitch. When you reach the end, you should have only one loop.
8. Step 8: Cut the NEXT loop free so that you have an extra piece of yarn. Pull the piece of yarn up through the loop and pull tight.

9. Step 9: Weave the piece of yarn through the seam you've just knitted. Then turn the piece right side out.

10. Step 10: Thread a piece of regular yarn onto a darning needle. Starting at the seam of one open end, thread the needle and yarn through the loops all the way around the opening until you reach where you started.

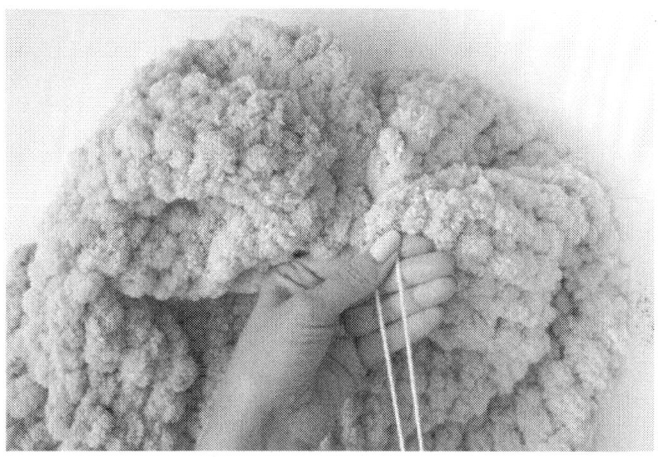

11. Step 11: Pull the yarn tight to pull the end of the pouf into a drawstring and tie tightly with multiple knots to secure.

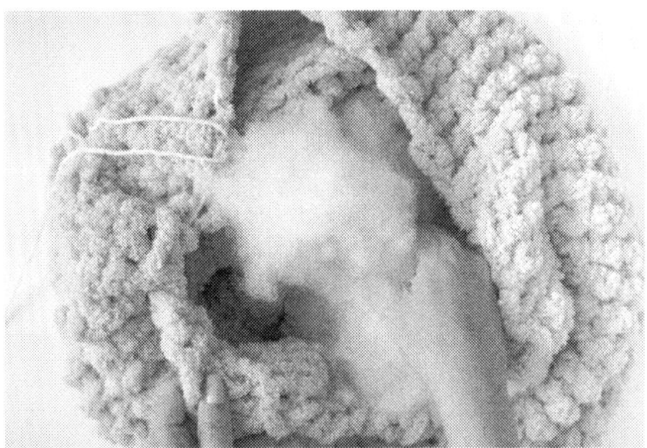

12. Step 12: Flip over to the other side and fill with fiberfill until very full. Repeat the drawstring at the open end and close tightly to finish the pouf!

Finger Knit Beanie

Materials

Super Chunky Wool (works best to make the beanie nice and chunky)

Pair of scissors

Your fingers

(in other words: you don't need much in order to finger knit a beanie!!)

Instructions

1. Step 1 : How to Finger Knit

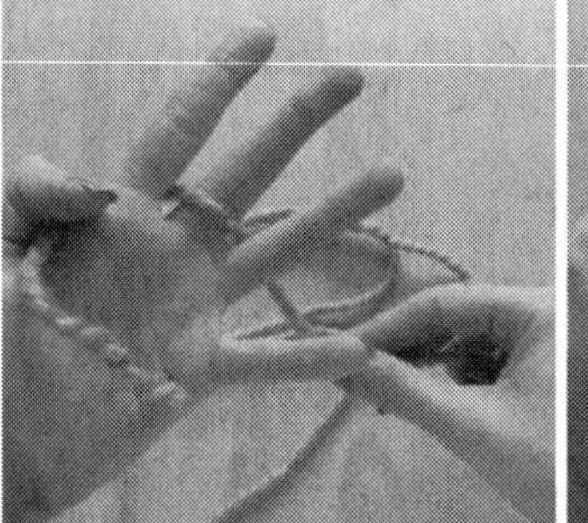
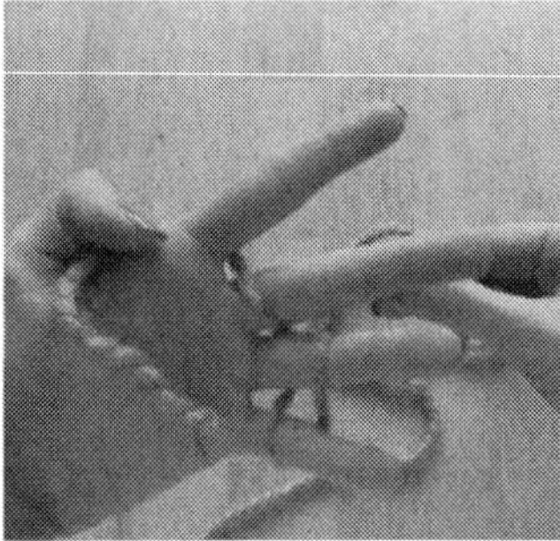

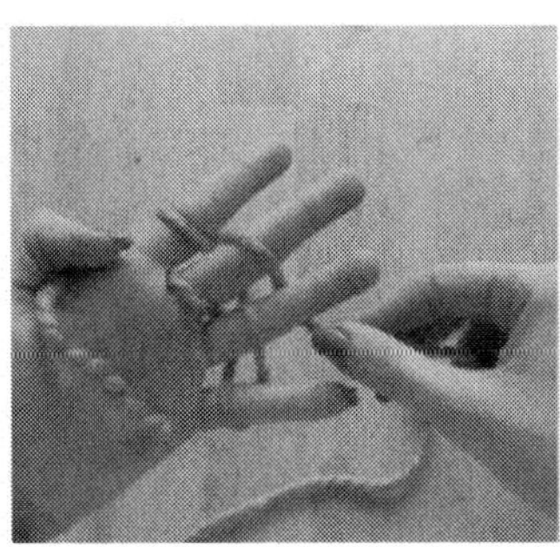
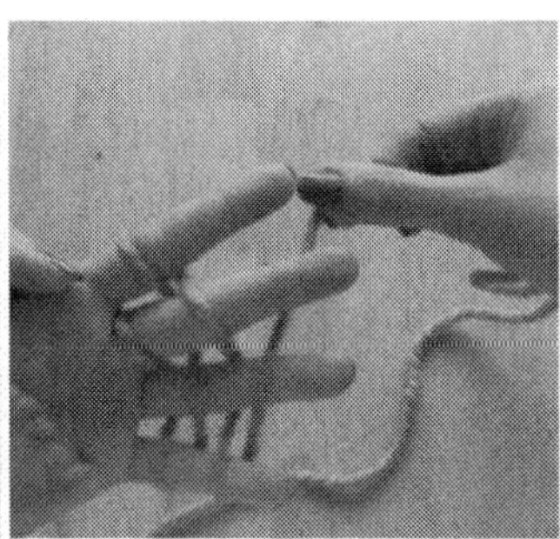

Hold the wool comfortably with your thumb.Wrap the wool behind your index finger and in front of your middle finger. Then behind your wedding finger and around your pinky. Then in front of your wedding finger, behind your middle finger and around your index finger.

You need to do it again. Wrap the wool in front of your middle finger. Behind your index finger. Then around your pinky. In front of your wedding finger, behind your middle finger and then around your index finger. So you have two loops on each finger.

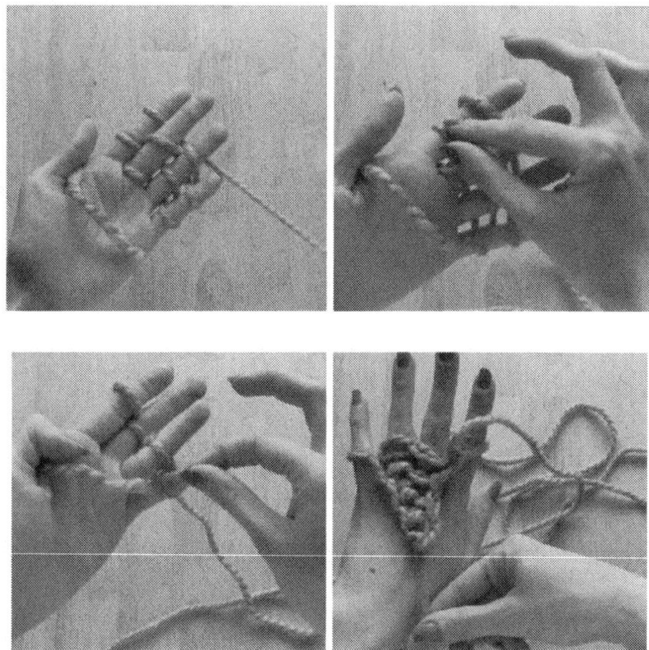

Now you need to pull the bottom loop up and over the top loop. On all fingers So you're left with one loop on each finger. Then start again. Keep repeating these steps until you have a long enough piece. Long enough to wrap around your head.

The next step I show how I connect the piece together to make a circular shape to form the hat. I also show how I continue to knit on. Connecting the knitting together as I go. Adding height to the beanie.

2. Step 2 : How to connect strands of your beanie hat

Now we are going to connect the two ends together. Run your thumb through the ridge on the back.The ridge is the back and the reverse side is the front.

Facing the ridged side in towards the center. Making sure you don't twist it. Connect the two together by hooking your little finger into the bottom loop and the top loop of the end of the knitted piece.So you have three loops on your little finger.

Then start knitting again as normal. When you start to pull loops off your finger, just one thing. On your pinky finger, pull each loop up and over individually.

Leaving one loop. Give it a tighten by pulling on the wool.

This stage is similar to the last step. I hook into each loop along the ridge of the knitted piece with my little finger. With two loops hooked on my finger I simply start to knit again I repeat this process. Adding more rows and height to the beanie hat. Measuring off my own head.

3. Step 3 : How to add a row to your finger knitted beanie hat DIY

This time we only need to hook into one loop. Find your next loop and hook your little finger into it. Then knit another row. On the little finger. Pull each loop off individually. Pull to tighten. Find your next loop and hook into it. Knit another row across. Keep knitting until the hat covers your head. Remember to keep trying on the hat for measurements.

The next stage I show how to decrease the size of the hat. To form the dome shape of the top of your beanie. After I measured off my head and I am happy with the height. Take up two loops this time, as appose to one. Continuing until you are left with a tiny gap at the top.

4. Step 4 : How to decrease

Next stage is to make the top of your hat. We need to start decreasing. This time you need to pick up two loops. So you have three loops on your little finger.

Then start to knit another row. Keep repeating these steps until the top of your hat is almost closed. Leaving a small gap.

This final stage – Casting off your fingers and how I close off the top of the beanie hat

5. Step 5: How to decrease and finish your beanie

Start casting off your fingers. Pull the first loop off and onto your next finger. And pull the bottom loop up and over the top. Do this on all your fingers.Until you have one left. Then pull the wool through the last loop. Get a scissors and cut the loop. To close off the top. I laced through each loop across the top. Keeping it nice and tight. Closing the top off completely. Make sure you keep pulling tight. You need to tie a knot in the wool to finish.

Finger Knit Statement Necklace

Materials

fabric yarn in an interesting print

fabric yarn in a contrasting solid

scissors

Instructions

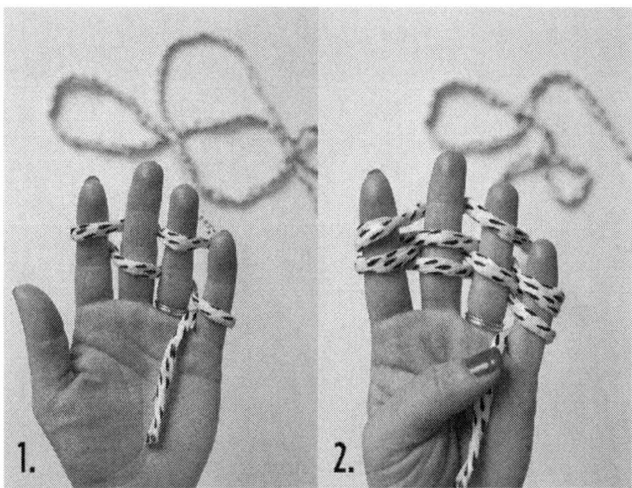

1. Tuck your end between your ring and pinky fingers and wrap it around your pinky finger and under your ring finger. Then wrap it over your middle finger, under and around your pointer finger, under your middle finger, and over your ring finger. These are your first two weft rows. Just like weaving!
2. Wrap around your pinky finger, under your ring finger, over your middle finger, under and around your pointer finger, back under your middle finger, and over your ring finger where you'll let your yarn hang down. These are your third and fourth weft rows.

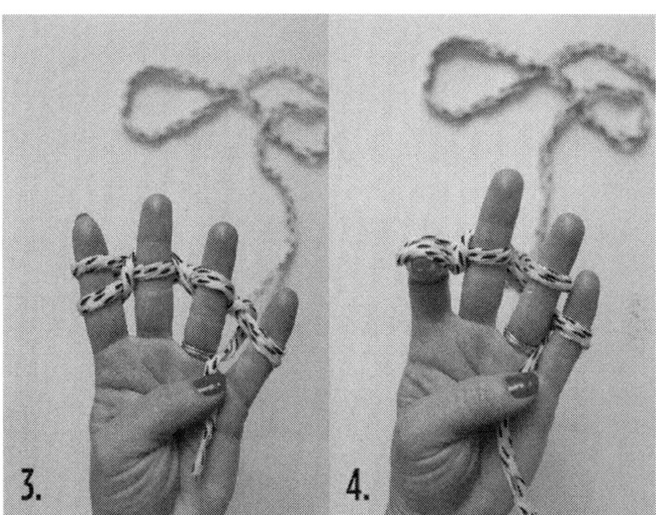

3. Put your thumb on top of your tail end to keep it from flying away. With your other hand, pull the bottom row on your pinky over the top of your finger. Your tail end will be part of that. Hold tight. Move to the ring finger and pull the bottom row up and over the top of your finger. Repeat with your middle finger.
4. You may need to bend your fingers down a bit as you pull the rows over the top.

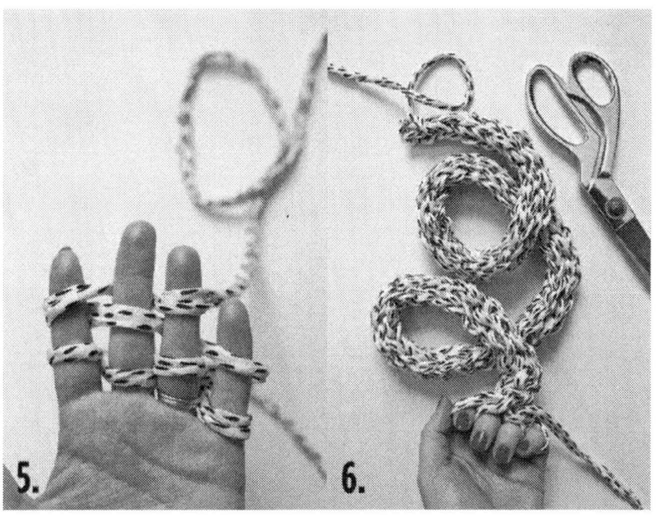

5. Add another two weft rows by wrapping the long end of your yarn around your pinky, under your ring finger, over your middle finger, under and around your pointer finger, back under your middle finger, and over your ring finger. Repeat the process of pulling the new bottom row up and over the new top row. Pull the tail to the back of your hand and pull down snuggly so that it forms a bit of a tight spot. You'll tie a knot here later.
6. Keep this up for maybe thirty minutes while listening to a podcast or chatting with a friend. Pull at the tail every few rows to help your garland curl into a rope. For this necklace design, you'll want about 33" of garland (not counting the tail).

7. When you're ready to end your garland, cut a tail about 6" long and weave it through each loop on each finger. Pull tightly.
8. Tie a single knot to secure each end of your garland.

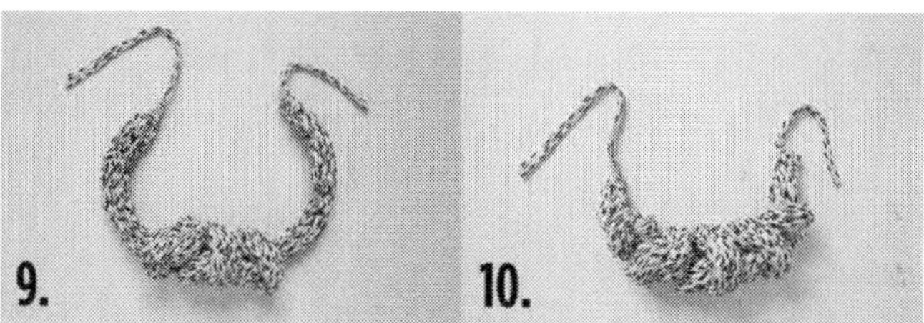

9. Tie three large but semi-loose knots in the center of your garland.
10. Tie a slightly tighter knot on each side of these three knots. You'll want to make sure they're all knotted in the same direction so you may have to work backwards on the left side knots.

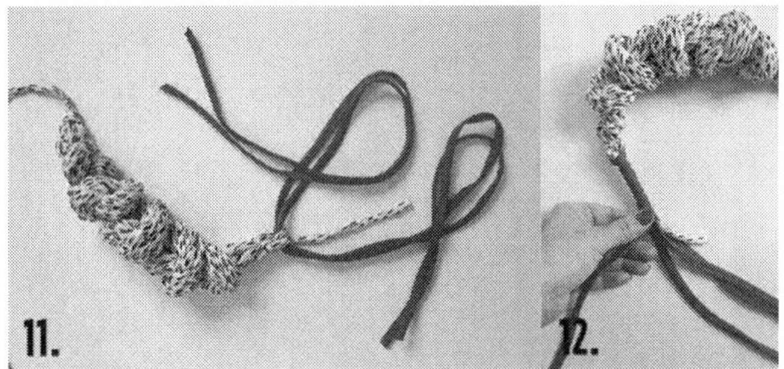

11. Cut two lengths of solid colored fabric yarn measuring about 3' each. Loop them through two loops under the knot at one end of your garland and make sure they're centered.
12. Wrap one of the strands of your solid yarn around the other three strands as well as the tail end of your printed yarn. Wrap tightly as you work and stop after you've wrapped about 4" long.

13. Tie all four strands into a knot and trim the two shorter ends. Gently pull your yarn over the cut ends to hide them. Repeat on the other side. Trim your loose ends so they're even and tie them together in a loose knot. Fabric yarn is so forgiving when trying to untie, but you can also pull this gently over your head every time since it's

got some stretch to it.

14. Enjoy your very own unique necklace that will upgrade any ensemble. These make great gifts for friends as well!

Finger Knit Infinity Scarf

Materials

Yarn

Scissors

Fingers

Instructions

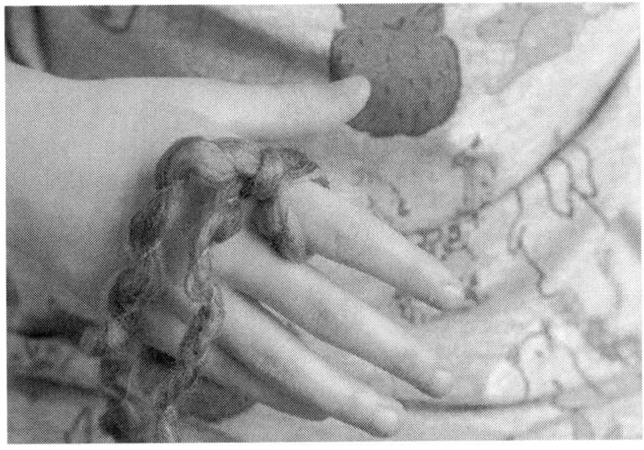

1. Make a slip knot and place on your index finger of your non-dominant hand (if you are right handed this will be your left hand and vice versa).

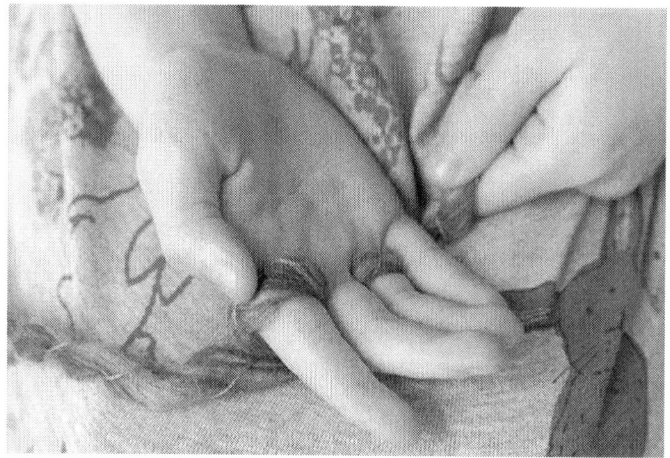

2. Weave the yarn behind your middle finger, in front of your ring finger and behind your little finger. Make sure you don't wrap the yarn too tightly, you don't want to cut off circulation in your fingers!!

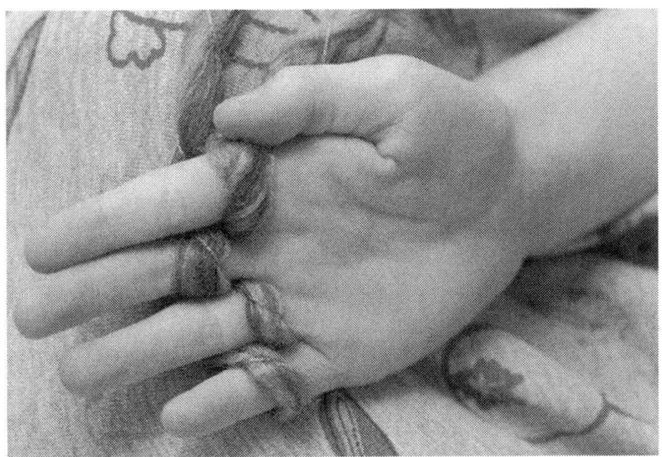

3. Weave the yarn back towards your thumb by continuing around in front of the little finger, behind your ring finger, in front of your middle finger and behind the index finger. You now have 1 complete row of loops.

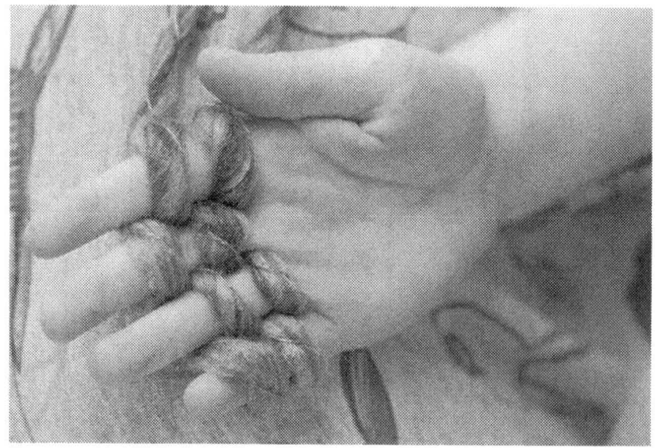

4. Continue the yarn around in front of your index finger and repeat steps 2 & 3 to complete a second row of loops.

5. Simply lift the bottom row of loops over the top row towards the back of your hand. You have now made your first line of finger knitting!

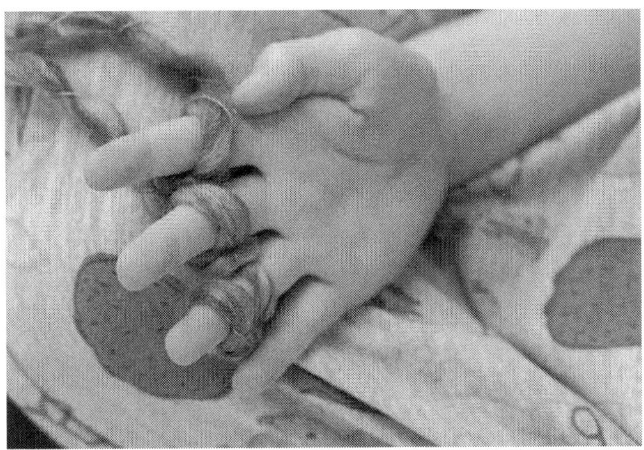

6. When your knitting is as long as you need for your project (we made ours 70" long). You need to finish off the end of the scarf. Transfer the loop from the little finger onto the ring finger and then pull the bottom loop over the top loop as you have been doing whilst knitting. Now transfer the loop from the ring finger onto the middle finger and again pull the bottom loop over the top loop. Transfer the loop from the middle finger to the index finger and pull the bottom loop over the top.

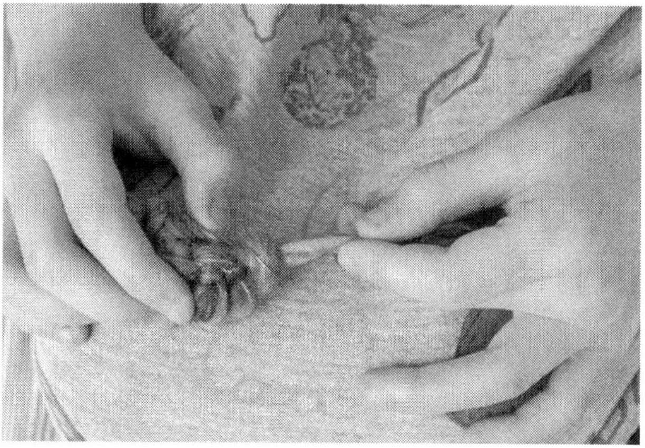

7. You now just have one loop remaining, which is on the index finger. Leaving a long tail, cut the yarn. Take the loop carefully off of your index finger and thread the tail through the loop and tighten.

8. Tie or sew the two ends of the scarf together!

Finger Knit Butterflies

Materials:

Yarn – doubled up worsted weight or a bulky yarn

Pipe Cleaners

Pencil

Instructions

1. Begin by finger knitting two separate ropes of yarn. For one start with 120 inches and for the other rope use a 70 inch long piece of yarn. These will be the wings of the butterfly. Ropes will vary in size a bit depending on the size of fingers and the weight of the yarn used.

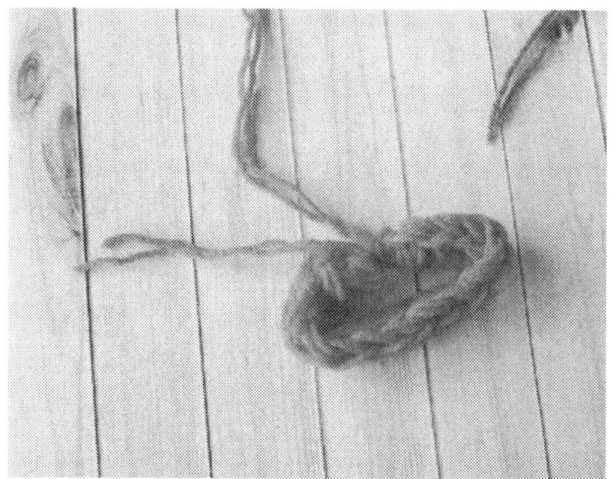

2. You can use the same color yarn for both wings, or do two different colors. Don't pull the chain tightly after it's done. You can kind of pull on it to shape it but don't tug to hard, just a little.

3. Once you have the wings of your butterfly finger knit, finish them off and tie the two ends together in a circle. Knot yarn.

4. Stack the two small circles on top of each other.

5. Wrap the yarn tail around the centers. Tie tightly to create wings. Tie the top to create a hanging hook or cut off if you don't want to hang the butterfly.

6. Fold a pipe cleaner in half and wrap around the butterfly in the center. Twist the top.

7. Use a pencil or marker to roll the pipe cleaner to create round antennae.

Finger-Knit Wreath

Materials

Two styrofoam wreaths. (The ones I found at Michaels weren't round, so I just put two of their forms together)

150 yards of chunky yarn to make a whole lotta finger knitting

24 gauge floral wire

Instructions

1. You need to begin by finger knitting your yarn. Here is a step-by-step finger-knitting how-to. Kids are great at it and it is a fun project for them to do while listening to a book read out loud. Read A Christmas Carol by Charles Dickens while you do it and your family will remember it for years to come. You will likely have to do more than one ball of yarn, but I show you how to join them below.
2. Next, you need to thread the floral wire through your strand of finger-knitting. This is much faster than it sounds so don't let it stop you. Make a loop and twist in the wire so it is easier to thread without getting caught on the yarn.

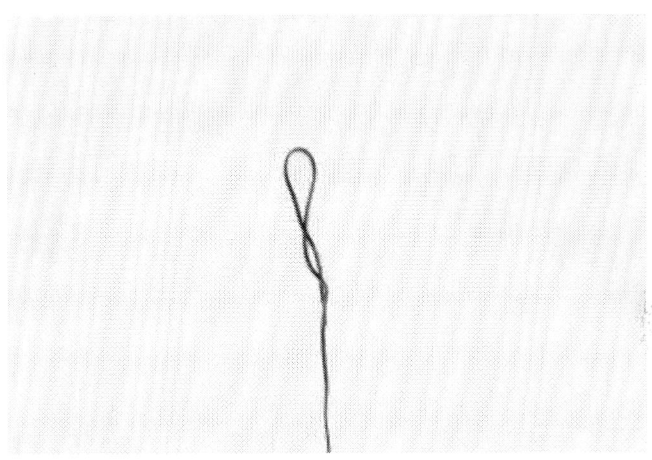

3. Thread the floral wire through the strand by going underneath one strand per row. Don't cut the wire yet.

4. For ease, you may want to work with the finger knitting bunched on the wire and then stretch it out as you apply it to the wreath. For this you need the amount of wire to be flexible.

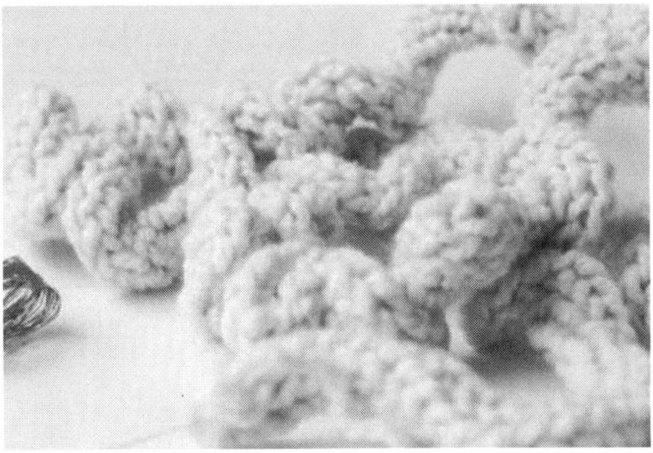

5. I simply held two wreath forms together, flat sides facing. If you found a round one, that that will work on its own.
6. Begin by wrapping a length of wire around the forms. wrapping in the strand from the end of your finger-knitting. The paddle with the wire should be at the other end.

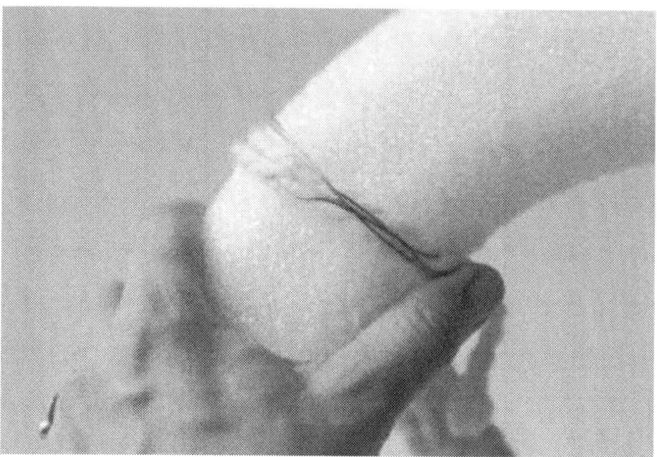

7. Start wrapping the strands around the form, pulling the strand tautly, but not too tightly on the wire. In the beginning this is a little more challenging because you have to pull the entire mess through the middle. I tried making a ball of it and pulling it through, but it just ended up twisting the strand too much. It won't take long before it's more manageable.

8. Condense the strands on the inner side of the ring as you go.
9. It should look like this.

10. Once you get to the end of your strand, cut the wire, leaving about 8 inches extra wire.
11. To join two strands, thread the wire from the end of the strand around your wreath into your new, already-wired-strand.

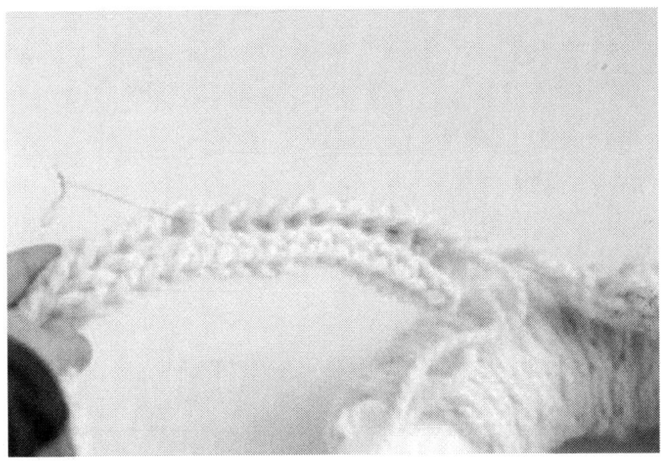

12. Thread the wire about six to eight inches in and twist the end around the wire that is already there. Repeat this process with the wire from the new strand into the old strand.
13. Then, thread the yarn ends of the finger knitting chain through the strand in the same way.

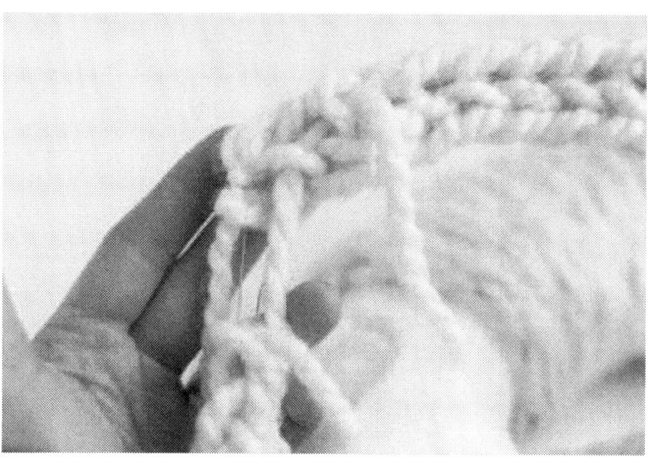

14. Pull tightly together and continue wrapping.
15. When you get back to the beginning, and you still have wired finger knitting left, hold it about where it would turn around the inside of the wreath.
16. Cut the strand an inch or so below that point.

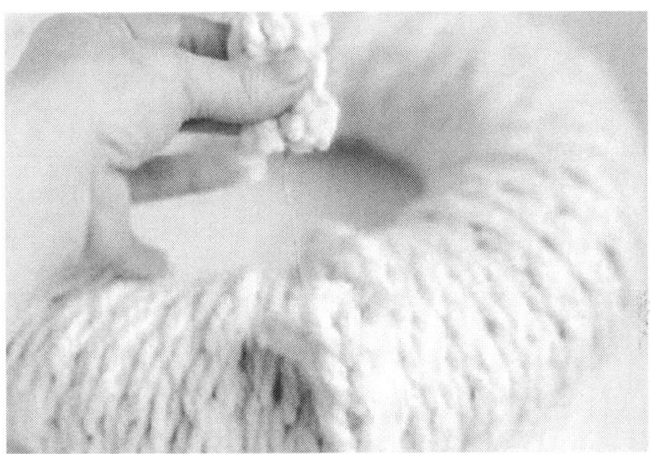

17. Pull out the extra little bits of cut finger knitting until you have the four loops (the ones that would be around your fingers). As you pull out a row or two you'll get a length of yarn again. Thread the loose yarn that you've pulled out through the four loops as if you were ending a strand of finger-knitting.

18. Twist and weave the end through the back of your wreath.
19. I did it such that there was a bit of hanging thread left, that I wove to come out the top of the wreath–perfect for hanging.

20. Voila! You're done.

21. I especially love it with that long green ribbon with long tails. I only had one length of that ribbon, and I wanted to hang them on the doors, so I had to cut it in half

Diy Finger Knit Yarn Gift Bows

Materials

Bernat Roving Wool in Rice Paper

Tape

Instructions

1. Finger Knitting with two fingers:

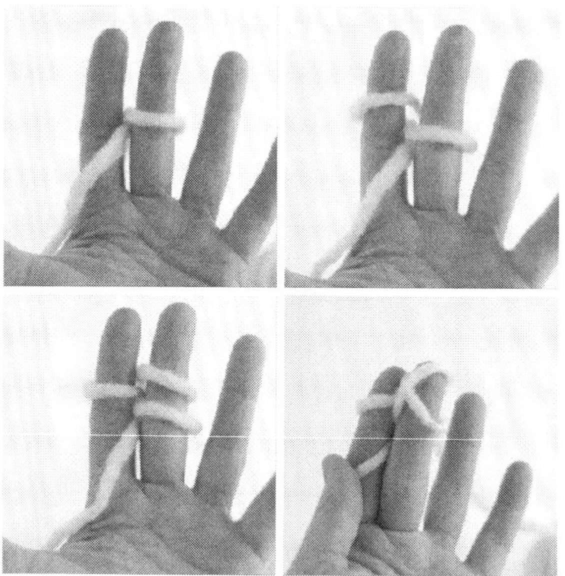

2. Bring wool over your forefinger and around your middle finger, leaving an 8" tail hanging between your thumb and forefinger.
3. Wrap yarn around your forefinger.
4. Bring yarn under and around your middle finger (you will now have two strands across each finger, including the tail of the yarn).

5. Lift the lower strand on your middle finger over the upper strand.
6. Bring the tail between your middle finger and forefinger.

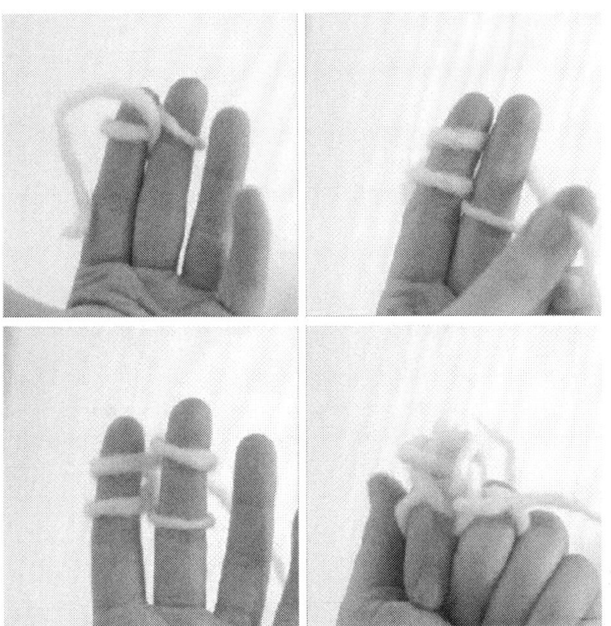

7. Wrap the yarn around your forefinger and then, around middle finger again.
8. You should have two strands on your fingers again. Repeat lifting the lower strand over the upper strand on each finger, beginning with your middle finger.
9. Continue finger knitting until you have a strand that is about 1.75 yards.

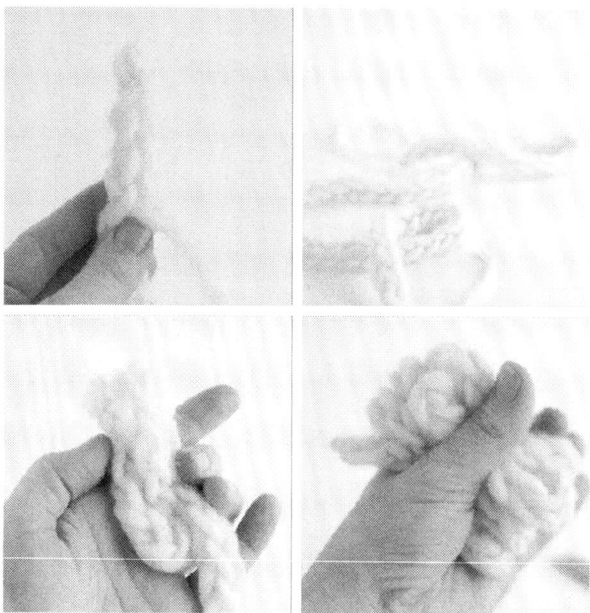

10. Finish off your strand when you have only 1 strand left on each finger. Cut the yarn about 10" from your hand and thread that tail under the fore finger strand and the middle finger strand. Tighten. Weave this end into the end of your strand.
11. Repeat this process for as many bows as you want to make.
12. Fold the strand back and forth in your hand in about 4" loops.
13. Make a good thick bundle in your hand with the finger knitted strand.

14. Take an extra piece of yarn and wrap around the middle of the bundle.
15. Then, form a loop in the yarn and bring it over the top of the bundle.
16. Repeat this a few times.
17. Tie off the yarn. Attach the finger knit yarn gift bows with a piece of tape to the top of each jar. Add a tag to your jar for easy giving. Or, use additional yarn to attach the bows to a package!

Finger Knit Letter Ornaments

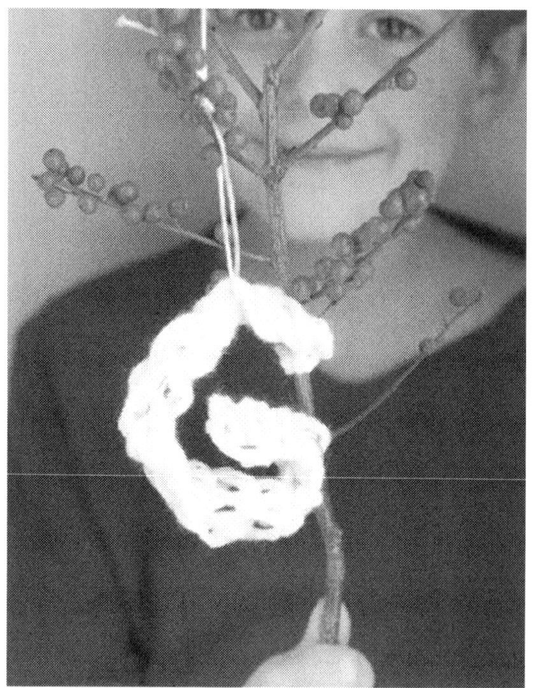

Materials

Length of Finger Knitting in white

White Pipe cleaner

Scissors

Instructions

1. Choose a length of complete finger knitting (how to finger know, here).
2. Thread pipe cleaner through the piece of finger knitting. Twist the pipe cleaners around the ends to secure.
3. Twist finger knitting into a letter form. Thread string through letter to hand and enjoy.

Finger Knitting Projects

Manufactured by Amazon.ca
Bolton, ON